2021 Copyright © Bahá'í International Community
(www.bahai.org)

Designed and Published by Simon Creedy
(simon@creedy.com.au)

O Friend!

In the garden of thy heart plant naught but the rose of love, and from the nightingale of affection and desire loosen not thy hold. Treasure the companionship of the righteous and eschew all fellowship with the ungodly.

–Bahá'u'lláh

BAHÁ'U'LLÁH

THE LIFE OF BAHÁ'U'LLÁH

Introduction ①

Early Life ②

Divine Revelation ④

Exile to Baghdad ⑥

Further Banishment ⑨

The Final Years ⑪

15 PRAYERS

⑮ – ㉜

THE GLORY OF GOD

The Shrine of Bahá'u'lláh, located in Bahjí near Acre, Israel, is the holiest place for Bahá'ís and represents their Qiblih, or direction of prayer. It contains the remains of Bahá'u'lláh and is near the spot where He died in the Mansion of Bahjí.

THE LIFE OF BAHÁ'U'LLÁH

INTRODUCTION

April, 1863. Men and women, young and old, from all walks of life, gathered on the thoroughfare leading to the banks of the River Tigris in Baghdad to bid a tearful farewell to One Who had become their friend, their comforter and their guide.

Mirza Husayn-'Alí–known as Bahá'u'lláh–was being banished from their midst. As a prominent follower of the Báb, whose teachings had swept through Persia two decades before, Bahá'u'lláh had forfeited the privileged life into which He had been born, and instead embraced imprisonment and exile for the rest of His days.

But despair would soon be transformed into hope: Before leaving the environs of Baghdad, Bahá'u'lláh would announce to His companions what many of them had already suspected–that He was the great Divine Educator heralded by the Báb, the initiator of a new era in history in which the tyrannies and injustices of the past would give way to a world of peace and justice: an embodiment of the principle of the oneness of humankind.

The "Divine Springtime," He would unequivocally proclaim, had arrived.

EARLY LIFE

Born in Tehran, Iran on 12 November, 1817, Mirza Husayn-'Alí enjoyed all the advantages conferred by noble birth. From a very early age, He displayed extraordinary knowledge and wisdom.

As a young man, rather than pursuing a career in government service as His father had done, Mirza Husayn-'Alí chose to devote His energies to the care of the poor. He showed no interest in seeking position or prominence.

With His acceptance of the religion of the Báb, life permanently changed for the young nobleman and His family. Although They never met in person, from the moment Mirza Husayn-'Alí heard of the Báb's message, He declared His wholehearted belief in it and put all of His energy and influence into promoting it.

In 1848, a significant gathering of the Báb's followers took place in a village in the northeast of Iran named Badasht. Mirza Husayn-'Alí played a central role in the proceedings, which affirmed the independent character of the new religion. From this time onwards, Mirza Husayn-'Alí was known as Bahá'u'lláh, meaning the "Glory of God" in Arabic.

As the community of the Báb's followers grew, so did the fierce opposition it provoked. Thousands upon thousands were subjected to the most cruel and barbaric treatment, and many were put to death. When three hundred Bábís sought refuge in a deserted shrine called Shaykh Tabarsi, Bahá'u'lláh set out to join them, but He was prevented from reaching His destination.

In 1850, the Báb was publicly executed. With the majority of the Báb's leading supporters killed, it soon became evident that Bahá'u'lláh was the only One to Whom the remaining Bábís could turn.

The city of Tehran, Iran, where Bahá'u'lláh was born.

DIVINE REVELATION

In 1852, Bahá'u'lláh was falsely charged with complicity in an attempt on the life of Nasiruddin Shah, the King of Iran. When the warrant was issued, He set out to face His accusers, much to the astonishment of those who were charged with arresting Him. They conducted Him, barefoot and in chains, through teeming streets to a notorious subterranean dungeon, known as the "Black Pit."

The dungeon had once been the reservoir for a public bath. Within its walls, prisoners languished in the cold and unhealthy air, clamped together by an unbearably heavy chain that left its mark on Bahá'u'lláh's body for the rest of His life.

It was in this grim setting that the rarest and most cherished of events was once again played out: a mortal man, outwardly human in every respect, was chosen by God to bring to humanity a new message.

This experience of Divine Revelation, touched on only indirectly in surviving accounts of the lives of Moses, Christ, and Muhammad, is illustrated in Bahá'u'lláh's own words:

"During the days I lay in the prison of Tihran, though the galling weight of the chains and the stench-filled air allowed Me but little sleep, still in those infrequent moments of slumber I felt as if something flowed from the crown of My head over My breast, even as a mighty torrent that precipitateth itself upon the earth from the summit of a lofty mountain... At such moments My tongue recited what no man could bear to hear."

Bahá'u'lláh describes Divine Revelation in His own words

EXILE TO BAGHDAD

After four months of intense suffering, Bahá'u'lláh–now ill and utterly exhausted–was released and exiled forever from His native Iran. He and His family were sent to Baghdad. There, the remaining followers of the Báb increasingly turned to Bahá'u'lláh for moral and spiritual guidance. The nobility of His character, the wisdom of His counsel, the kindness that He showered upon all and the increasing evidences of superhuman greatness in Him, revived the downtrodden community.

Bahá'u'lláh's emergence as the leader of the community of the Báb's followers increasingly aroused the intense jealousy of Mirza Yahya, His ambitious, younger half-brother. Mirza Yahya made several shameless efforts to slander Bahá'u'lláh's character and sow seeds of suspicion and doubt among His companions. To remove Himself from being the cause of tension, Bahá'u'lláh retired to the mountains of Kurdistan, where He remained for two years, reflecting on His divine purpose. This period of His life was reminiscent of Moses' withdrawal to Mount Sinai, Christ's days in the wilderness, and Muhammad's retreat in the Arabian hills.

Yet even in this remote region, Bahá'u'lláh's fame spread. People heard that a man of extraordinary wisdom and eloquence was to be found there. When such stories reached Baghdad, the Bábís, guessing Bahá'u'lláh's identity, dispatched a mission to implore Him to return.

Residing once more in Baghdad, Bahá'u'lláh reinvigorated the Báb's followers; the stature of the community grew and His reputation spread ever further. He composed three of His most renowned works at this time–the Hidden Words, the Seven Valleys and the Book of Certitude (Kitáb-i-Íqán). While Bahá'u'lláh's writings alluded to His station, it was not yet the time for a public announcement.

As Bahá'u'lláh's fame spread, the envy and malice of some of the clergy was rekindled. Representations were made to the Shah of Iran to ask the Ottoman Sultan to remove Bahá'u'lláh further from the Iranian border. A second banishment was decreed.

Taj belonging to Bahá'u'lláh

At the end of April 1863, shortly before leaving the environs of Baghdad for Istanbul (known as Constantinople in the English language of the time), Bahá'u'lláh and His companions resided for twelve days in a garden which He named Ridván, meaning "Paradise". There, on the banks of the River Tigris, Bahá'u'lláh declared Himself to be the One heralded by the Báb–God's Messenger to the age of humanity's collective maturity, foretold in all the world's scriptures.

A modern view of the house of Rida Big, the residence of Bahá'u'lláh in Adrianople for one year. The Mosque of Sultan Salim is in the background.

FURTHER BANISHMENT

Three months after departing Baghdad, Bahá'u'lláh and His fellow exiles reached Constantinople. They remained there for just four months before a further banishment took them to Edirne (Adrianople), a gruelling journey undertaken during the coldest of winters. In Adrianople, their accommodation failed to protect them from the bitter temperatures.

Bahá'u'lláh referred to Adrianople as the "remote prison." Yet despite the inhospitable conditions under which the exiles were forced to live, inspired verses continued to flow from Bahá'u'lláh's pen, and His message reached as far away as Egypt and India.

During this period Mirza Yahya, the jealous half-brother of Bahá'u'lláh, contrived to poison Him. This tragic episode left Bahá'u'lláh with a tremor that showed in His handwriting to the end of His life.

Beginning in September 1867, Bahá'u'lláh wrote a series of letters to the leaders and rulers of various nations. In these prescient writings, He openly proclaimed His station, speaking of the dawn of a new age. But first, He warned, there would be catastrophic upheavals in the world's political and social order. He summoned the world's leaders to uphold justice and called upon them to convene an assembly where they would meet and put an end to war. Only by acting collectively, He said, could a lasting peace be established. His warnings fell upon deaf ears.

Continued agitation from Bahá'u'lláh's detractors caused the Ottoman government to banish Him one final time, to its most notorious penal colony. Arriving in the Mediterranean prison city of 'Akká on 31 August 1868, Bahá'u'lláh was to spend the rest of His life in the fortified city and its environs.

Confined to a prison for more than two years, He and His companions were later moved to a cramped house within the city's walls. Little by little, the moral character of the

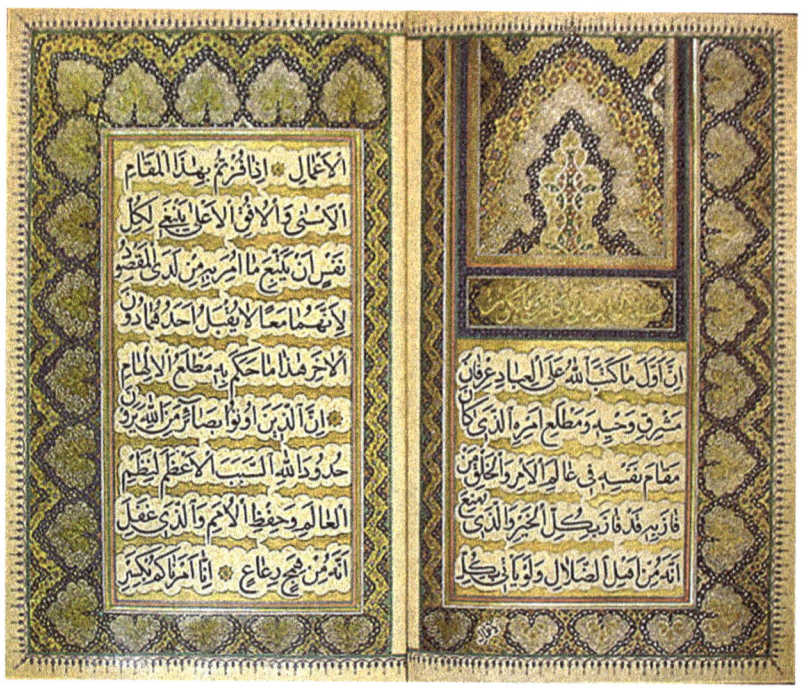

An illuminated copy of the Kitáb-i-Aqdas, commissioned by 'Abdu'l-Bahá in 1902.

Bahá'ís–particularly Bahá'u'lláh's eldest son, 'Abdu'l-Bahá–softened the hearts of their jailers, and penetrated the bigotry and indifference of 'Akká's residents. As in Baghdad and Adrianople, the nobility of Bahá'u'lláh's character gradually won the admiration of the community at large, including some of its leaders.

In 'Akká, Bahá'u'lláh revealed His most important work, the Kitáb-i-Aqdas (the Most Holy Book), in which He outlined the essential laws and principles of His Faith, and established the foundations for a global administrative order.

THE FINAL YEARS

In the late 1870s, Bahá'u'lláh–while still a prisoner–was granted some freedom to move outside of the city's walls, allowing His followers to meet with Him in relative peace. In April 1890, Professor Edward Granville Browne of Cambridge University met Bahá'u'lláh at the mansion near 'Akká where He had taken up residence.

Browne wrote of their meeting: "The face of Him on Whom I gazed I can never forget, though I cannot describe it. Those piercing eyes seemed to read one's very soul; power and authority sat on that ample brow... No need to ask in whose presence I stood, as I bowed myself before one who is the object of a devotion and love which kings might envy and emperors sigh for in vain."

Bahá'u'lláh passed away on 29 May, 1892. In His will, He designated 'Abdu'l-Bahá as His successor and Head of the Bahá'í Faith – the first time in history that the Founder of a world religion had named his successor in a written irrefutable text. This choice of a successor is a central provision of what is known as the "Covenant of Bahá'u'lláh," enabling the Bahá'í community to remain united for all time.

The Mansion of Mazra'ih — one of the homes where Bahá'u'lláh stayed after being released from the prison city of 'Akká.

O Son of Spirit!

With the joyful tidings of light I hail thee: rejoice! To the court of holiness I summon thee; abide therein that thou mayest live in peace forevermore.

–Bahá'u'lláh

BAHÁ'U'LLÁH

15 Prayers

THE GLORY OF GOD

O God, my God!

I yield Thee thanks for having guided me unto Thy straight Path and enabled me to recognize Thee and turn unto Thee, and for having made known unto me the oneness of Thine Essence and the sanctity of Thy Being. I implore Thee, by them Who are the Daysprings of Thy Cause, the Dawning-Places of Thy grace, and the Repositories of Thy knowledge and wisdom, to bless the gift which Thou hast bestowed upon me through Thy bounty and favour. Do Thou ordain for me and for her mother, as well as for her, the good of this world and of the next. Thou art, verily, the Lord of all being, Who hearest and art ready to answer.[1]

–Bahá'u'lláh

[1] *Revealed for the recipient on the occasion of the birth of his daughter*

Praise be to Thee, O my God, that Thou didst graciously remember me through Thy Most Exalted Pen, at a time when Thou wert held in the Most Great Prison by reason of that which the hands of such enemies as had turned away from Thee and from Thy most resplendent signs had wrought. O my Lord! I have turned unto Thee and have set my face towards Thy Horizon. I beseech Thee, by the wrongs which He Who is the Dayspring of Thy signs and the Dawning-Place of Thy clear tokens hath suffered, to ordain for me what will profit me in every world of Thy worlds. Thou, verily, knowest me better than I know myself. Thou art the All-Knowing, the All-Informed.

I entreat Thee, moreover, O Lord of all being and Possessor of all things visible and invisible, to bestow upon me a righteous child who may make mention of Thee on Thine earth and sing Thy praise throughout Thy realms; this, notwithstanding that Thou hast, with this Tablet, made me rich enough to dispense with every fruit, trace, or mention. I close my supplication, at this moment, with that which one of Thy chosen ones hath aforetime spoken: "O my Lord, leave me not childless, even though there is no better heir than Thyself."[1]

–Bahá'u'lláh

[1] Qur'án 21:89

He is the Ever-Abiding, the Almighty, the Most High.

Glory be to Thee, O Lord my God! I implore Thee by this Name that hath been hemmed in by tribulations on every side and assailed by afflictions from every direction, in such wise that He findeth none to help Him on Thine earth or to succour Him in Thy dominion, to ease the pangs of labour for this handmaiden and guard her therefrom, and to free her from this pain and change it into comfort and relief. Potent art Thou to do what Thou willest, and able to ordain what Thou pleasest. Thou art, verily, the Almighty, the Incomparable, the Ever-Forgiving, the Most Compassionate.

–Bahá'u'lláh

Pure and sanctified art Thou, O my God!

How can the pen move and the ink flow after the breezes of loving-kindness have ceased, and the signs of bounty have vanished, when the sun of abasement hath risen, and the swords of calamity are drawn, when the heavens of sorrow have been upraised, and the darts of affliction and the lances of vengeance have rained from the clouds of power – in such wise that the signs of joy have departed from all hearts, and the tokens of gladness have been erased from every horizon, the gates of hope have been shut, the mercy of the supernal breeze hath ceased to waft over the rose-garden of faithfulness, and the whirlwind of extinction hath struck the tree of existence. The pen is groaning, and the ink bewaileth its plight, and the tablet is awestruck at this cry. The mind is in turmoil from the taste of this pain and sorrow, and the divine Nightingale calleth: "Alas! Alas! for all that hath been made to appear." And this, O my God, is from naught but Thy hidden bounties.

–Bahá'u'lláh

O Thou Who holdest within Thy grasp the Kingdom of names and the Empire of all things, Thou seest how I have become a stranger from my land on account of my love for Thee.

I beg of Thee, by the beauty of Thy countenance, to make my remoteness from home a means whereby Thy servants may be drawn nigh unto the Fountain-head of Thy Cause and the Dayspring of Thy Revelation. O God, I call on Thee with a tongue that hath spoken no word of disobedience against Thee, imploring Thee, by Thy sovereignty and might, to keep me safe in the shelter of Thy mercy and to grant me strength to serve Thee and to serve my father and mother. Thou, verily, art the Almighty, the Help in Peril, the Self-Subsisting.

–Bahá'u'lláh

In the Name of our Lord, the Most Holy, the Most Great, the Exalted, the Most Glorious!

Glory be to Thee, O Thou Who art the Lord of all beings and the Ultimate Aim of all creation! I testify with the tongue of both mine inner and outer being that Thou hast revealed and manifested Thyself, that Thou hast sent down Thy verses and demonstrated Thy proofs, and that Thou art independent of anyone besides Thee and sanctified above all else except Thyself. I ask Thee, by the glory of Thy Cause and the power of Thy Word, graciously to assist them that have arisen to discharge what hath been enjoined upon them in Thy Book, and to perform that whereby the fragrance of Thine acceptance may be shed abroad. Thou, verily, art the Powerful, the Gracious, the Forgiving, the Bountiful.

—Bahá'u'lláh

In the Name of our Lord, the Most Holy, the Most Great, the Exalted, the Most Glorious!

O God, my God! Thou seest how Thy servant hath set his face towards Thee and desired to be honoured by performing that whereunto he hath been bidden in Thy Book. Do Thou ordain for him through Thy Most Exalted Pen that which shall draw him nigh unto the Most Sublime Summit. Thou, verily, art the Educator of the world and the Lord of the nations, and Thou, verily, art the Potent, the All-Subduing, the Almighty.

–Bahá'u'lláh

O God, my God!

Glory be to Thee for having guided me unto the horizon of Thy Revelation, illumined me with the splendours of the light of Thy grace and mercy, caused me to speak forth Thy praise, and given me to behold that which hath been revealed by Thy Pen.

I beseech Thee, O Thou the Lord of the kingdom of names and Fashioner of earth and heaven, by the rustling of the Divine Lote-Tree and by Thy most sweet utterance which hath enraptured the realities of all created things, to raise me up in Thy Name amidst Thy servants. I am he who hath sought in the daytime and in the night season to stand before the door of Thy bounty and to present himself before the throne of Thy justice. O Lord! Cast not away him who hath clung to the cord of Thy nearness, and deprive not him who hath directed his steps towards Thy most sublime station, the summit of glory, and the supreme objective–that station wherein every atom crieth out in the most eloquent tongue, saying: "Earth and heaven, glory and dominion are God's, the Almighty, the All-Glorious, the Most Bountiful!"

–Bahá'u'lláh

Praise be to Thee, O Lord my God, for guiding me unto the horizon of Thy Revelation and for causing me to be mentioned by Thy Name. I beseech Thee, by the spreading rays of the Daystar of Thy providence and by the billowing waves of the Ocean of Thy mercy, to grant that my speech may bear a trace of the influence of Thine own exalted Word, attracting thereby the realities of all created things. Powerful art Thou to do what Thou willest through Thy wondrous and incomparable Utterance.

–Bahá'u'lláh

He is the Peerless!

Praise be unto Thee, O Lord my God! I beseech Thee by Thy Most Exalted Name in the Tabernacle of effulgent splendour, and by Thy Most Sublime Word in the Dominion of transcendent glory, to protect this servant, who hath enjoyed companionship with Thee, hearkened unto the accents of Thy voice and recognized Thy proof. Vouchsafe, then, unto him the good of both this world and the next, and grant unto him the station of righteousness in Thy presence, that his feet may not slip from Thine all-glorious and most exalted path.

–Bahá'u'lláh

He is the All-Glorious!

Praise be to Thee, O my God! Thou didst call me, and I answered Thee. Thou didst summon me, and I hastened unto Thee, entering beneath the shade of Thy mercy and seeking shelter at the threshold of the door of Thy grace. Thou hast nurtured me, O Lord, through Thy providence, chosen me for Thee alone, created me for Thy service, and appointed me to stand before Thee. I beseech Thee, by Thine all-glorious Name and by Thy beauty that hath dawned above the horizon of Thy most exalted Essence, to cause me to be related to Thee even as Thou hadst done so aforetime, and not to separate me from Thyself. Cause then to appear from me, O my God, that which is worthy of Thee. Thou art, in truth, powerful over all things.

–Bahá'u'lláh

O my God! O my God!

I testify that this is Thy Day which hath been mentioned in Thy Books, Thy Epistles, Thy Psalms and Thy Tablets. In it Thou hast manifested that which was hidden in Thy Knowledge and stored up in the repositories of Thine unfailing protection. I beseech Thee, O Lord of the world, by Thy Most Great Name whereby the limbs of the people were shaken, to assist Thy servants and Thy handmaidens to become steadfast in Thy Cause and to arise in Thy service.

Verily, Thou art potent to do whatsoever Thou willest, and in Thy grasp are the reins of all things. Thou protectest whomsoever Thou willest through Thy Power and Dominion. And verily, Thou art the Almighty, the All-Subduing, the Most Powerful.

–Bahá'u'lláh

In regard to his affairs, let him repeat nineteen times:

"Thou seest me, O my God, detached from all save Thee and cleaving unto Thee. Guide me, then, in all mine affairs unto that which profiteth me for the glory of Thy Cause and the loftiness of the station of Thy loved ones."

Let him then reflect upon the matter and undertake whatever cometh to mind. This vehement opposition of the enemies will indeed give way to supreme prosperity.

–Bahá'u'lláh

He is God, exalted is He, the Lord of might and grandeur!

O God, my God! I yield Thee thanks at all times and render Thee praise under all conditions.

In prosperity, all praise is Thine, O Lord of the Worlds, and in its absence, all gratitude is Thine, O Desire of them that have recognized Thee!

In adversity, all honour is Thine, O Adored One of all who are in heaven and on earth, and in affliction, all glory is Thine, O Enchanter of the hearts of those who yearn after Thee!

In hardship, all praise is Thine, O Thou the Goal of them that seek after Thee, and in comfort, all thanksgiving is Thine, O Thou whose remembrance is treasured in the hearts of those who are nigh unto Thee!

In wealth, all splendour is Thine, O Lord of them that are devoted to Thee, and in poverty, all command is Thine, O Thou the Hope of them that acknowledge Thy unity!

In joy, all glory is Thine, O Thou besides Whom there is none other God, and in sorrow, all beauty is Thine, O Thou besides Whom there is none other God!

In hunger, all justice is Thine, O Thou besides Whom there is none other God, and in satiety, all grace is Thine, O Thou besides Whom there is none other God!

In my homeland, all bounty is Thine, O Thou besides Whom there is none other God, and in exile, all decree is Thine, O Thou besides Whom there is none other God!

Under the sword, all munificence is Thine, O Thou besides Whom there is none other God, and in the safety of home, all perfection is Thine, O Thou besides Whom there is none other God!

In the lofty mansion, all generosity is Thine, O Thou besides Whom there is none other God, and upon the lowly dust, all favour is Thine, O Thou besides Whom there is none other God!

In prison, all fidelity is Thine, O Thou the Bestower of gifts, and in confinement, all eternity is Thine, O Thou Who art the ever-abiding King!

All bounty is Thine, O Thou Who art the Lord of bounty, and the Sovereign of bounty, and the King of bounty! I bear witness that Thou art to be praised in Thy doings, O Thou Source of bounty, and to be obeyed in Thy behests, O Thou Ocean of bounty, He from Whom all bounty doth proceed, He to Whom all bounty doth return!

–Bahá'u'lláh

Praised be Thou, O Lord my God!

Sanctify mine eye, and mine ear, and my tongue, and my spirit, and my heart, and my soul, and my body, and mine entire being from turning unto anyone but Thee. Give me then to drink from the cup that brimmeth with the sealed wine of Thy glory.

—Bahá'u'lláh

www.ingramcontent.com/pod-product-compliance
Lightning Source LLC
Chambersburg PA
CBHW040418100526
44588CB00022B/2867